Kitchen Garden Cookbook: *Tomatoes*

Jane McMorland Hunter

National Trust

To Sue Gibb

First published in the United Kingdom in 2011 by National Trust Books,
10 Southcombe Street, London W14 0RA

An imprint of Anova Books Company Ltd

ISBN 978 1 907892 01 1

A CIP catalogue record for this book is available from the British Library.

19 18 17 16 15 14 13 12
10 9 8 7 6 5 4 3 2 1

Reproduction by Mission Productions, Hong Kong
Printed and bound by 1010 Printing International, China

Acknowledgements

Louy Piachaud, Sue and David Gibb, Libby Kerr, Sally Hughes and Philip
Kelly have variously supplied recipes, tested them and tasted the
finished products. Without them, the recipe section would have been a
lot less interesting and wildly inaccurate. Grant Berry, the staff at the
National Trust gardens and the RHS library at Wisley made the research
fun and easy. At Anova Books, Tina Persaud, Nicola Newman and Komal
Patel have been brilliant to work with. My agent, Teresa Chris, has, as
always, been the perfect combination of inspiration and encouragement.
Tony Smith and everyone at Slightly Foxed coped brilliantly when my
potato obsession changed to tomatoes, for which I am very grateful.
Above all though, a huge thanks to Aimi Engineer for recipe ideas, route
planning, being interested in blight and so much more.

Contents

Introduction

Tomatoes are a close relative of deadly nightshade, yet delicious to eat; for years they were grown only as an ornamental; they are a fruit we treat as a vegetable – tomatoes are full of inconsistencies. Despite this, or perhaps because of it, they are one of the most popular plants to grow in a kitchen garden, in a greenhouse, or even on a window-sill. They are a food that really tastes different when home-grown. A tomato warmed by the sunshine and eaten fresh off the vine is so far removed from a pre-packed supermarket specimen that it is hard to believe they are the same fruit.

Although tomatoes come from South America, they have adapted well to life in Europe. Whether you live in the cool north or sheltered south, are using a greenhouse or planting outside, there is a variety that will suit almost any environment. There is even a variety that grows on the Galapagos Islands and is tolerant of salt water. Unfortunately, this development is less useful than it might at first seem, as the seeds will only germinate if they have passed through the digestive system of a giant turtle – and only a giant turtle will do.

In the kitchen, tomatoes are incredibly versatile, adding taste and colour to innumerable meals. You can eat them raw or cooked, they can be dried or frozen, or made into dishes as varied as salsa or sweet custard. One of the main reasons for growing your own is that you will get the truly fresh flavour that vanishes once tomatoes are packaged up for sale. Also, you will eat tomatoes when they are in season. Once we get into the middle of autumn in Britain, it is really not worth

Poma amoris fructu rubro.

buying fresh tomatoes. They may look fine, but the chances are they will taste of nothing. It is much better to rely on those you have stored, or to buy tinned tomatoes, many of which are now very good and are perfect for making comforting winter dishes: do you really want to eat salad when it is snowing outside?

Tomatoes can also be used to make your garden look attractive. They can be grown in a vegetable plot or in amongst flowers and will enhance any site. Tumbling varieties can be allowed to cascade out of baskets or over the edges of raised beds, bush tomatoes will provide upright structure all summer long, and cordons (the most common type of tomato plants) will climb to almost indefinite heights. As they ripen, many of the fruits are beautiful, with a wide range of colours, stripes and patterns. A few years ago, not many people would have thought to visit a garden to look at the vegetables, and even fewer would have expected to find vegetables and fruit in amongst the flowers. All that has changed now and many National Trust gardens have wonderful displays that are both functional and inspirational.

Tomatoes are the perfect crop to grow in a garden, fitting into almost any space and providing you with delicious meals throughout the year.

A brief history of tomatoes

Tomatoes originated in the lowlands of the Andes, an area covering parts of present-day Peru, Chile and Ecuador. The cherry-sized fruits grew wild on long, trailing vines and although people did eat them, no one made much effort to cultivate the plants. As people migrated, so the fruits spread and gradually the Mayan people domesticated them, concentrating on the larger fruits. The Aztecs grew tomatoes throughout their empire and introduced the word *tomatl*, which actually means 'plump fruit'; *xitomatl* means 'tomato' and *miltomatl* means 'tomatillo', but the Spanish conquistadores who conquered the region did not appreciate the difference between them and called both fruits 'tomato'.

Tomatoes arrive in Europe

In the fifteenth or sixteenth century, tomatoes arrived in Europe. It is not certain who brought them, but they first appeared in cultivation in Spain and had reached Italy by 1522, possibly via Morocco, accounting for their early Italian name, *pomi de Mori* or 'apples of the Moors'. They were recognised as close relatives of deadly nightshade and variously regarded as poison or aphrodisiac; the smell of the leaves and the brightness of the berries also aroused suspicion. In 1578, Rembert Dodoens's *A Niewe Herball, or Historie of Plants* described them as 'dangerous to be used' and for many years they were mostly grown in botanical collections or as ornamental plants.

7

The early tomatoes were bright yellow and spread slowly around Europe, but for the next 300 years they were really only eaten in Spain and Italy. In Italy they became known as *pomodoro*, possibly a variant of *pomi de Mori*, or possibly referring to their colouring (*pomo d'oro* or 'golden apples'). In France they became *pommes d'amour* ('apples of love') but took a long time to be included in recipes, and were still being listed as an ornamental in gardening catalogues as late as 1850. The earliest printed recipe for tomatoes is in a Neapolitan book, *Lo Scalo alla moderna*, dating from 1692-4, and is called Tomato Sauce, Spanish Style. Tomatoes took time to be accepted as food partly because they weren't mentioned in the Bible and partly because there was no particular need for them: they didn't replace anything, they were no good at filling the poor and hungry and, at first, they were very tart. They were also hard to grow in much of northern Europe, only suiting the warmer southern countries.

Red tomatoes take over

Red tomatoes were brought to Italy from Mexico by two Jesuit monks some time after the yellow ones and immediately became more popular. In the eighteenth century, the Neapolitan chef Francesco Leonardi combined tomatoes with pasta and meatballs, thus ensuring their lasting popularity. Peasant farmers liked growing tomatoes because, although labour-intensive, they were reliable over a long season and were a welcome addition to a predominantly green and brown, rather boring diet. Tomatoes provided entertainment as well, in the form of *pomodorato*, the throwing of tomatoes at below-standard public performers. This practice has largely died out, but every year in Spain there is a festival where the highlight of events is a huge street fight with tons of overripe tomatoes (see page 94).

Britain gets to know the tomato

Tomatoes were treated with grave suspicion when they first arrived in Britain. John Parkinson, King Charles I's herbalist, described them as 'full of a slimie juice and a waterie pulp'. In the second edition of his *Herball*, in 1636, John Gerard said 'They yeeld little nourishment to the body and same naught and corrupt' and in 1677 they were included (wrongly described as violet-coloured) in a 'dictionary of difficult terms' (Elisha Coles, *An English Dictionary Explaining the Difficult Terms that are used in Divinity, Husbandry, Physick, Philosophy, Law, Navigation, Mathematicks and Other Arts and Sciences*). Hannah Glasse, in her 1747 cookery book, only thought to include tomatoes in the supplement.

9

The British remained very cautious until the nineteenth century, with the Victorians using the spreading cordons to decorate trellises more often than to produce food. In the mid-1860s, all this changed when large-scale production under glass became possible, and the tomato suddenly appeared everywhere. It was one of the most popular crops for home gardeners, and small greenhouses sprang up in back gardens up and down the country. It was one of the first 'vegetables' to be eaten raw, and also became very popular grilled for breakfast.

At the same time, Guernsey tomatoes, popularly known as 'Guernsey Toms', appeared and dominated the UK market for much of the twentieth century. The tomatoes were originally grown as a catch crop in between the vines that the islanders grew for grapes to send to the mainland. By the First World War, tomatoes had taken over and expanded to such an extent that during busy times extra 'tomato trains' ran from Weymouth to London carrying the crop. Guernsey tomatoes are still grown on a large scale, but now the Netherlands is the leader in greenhouse technology, with thousands of hectares given over to closely monitored plants.

Tomato products

Ketchup, sauces and the canning industry ensured that people could eat tomatoes all year round. Tomato purée and ketchup had been made on a domestic scale around the Mediterranean for many years, but in 1830 the production of ketchup began in America, resulting in a product that now appears on tables worldwide. By the mid-nineteenth century, there were large-scale canning plants in America and later around Naples, preserving fruits of both good and poor quality.

HEINZ TOMATO KETCHUP

GM tomatoes

In the late twentieth century, genetically modified (GM) food began appearing. The Flavr Savr tomato was engineered so that its ripening gene would stop at a certain point, so the fruit would remain firm and have a longer shelf life. Other varieties have been modified to need less water or include higher levels of the cancer-fighting antioxidant lycopene.

Genetically modified tomatoes are now included in many purée, paste and chopped tomato products. Whether we like it or not, genetic modification is here to stay. At the moment, most GM tomatoes are grown in developing countries, but the tomato is one of the most suitable plants for genetic modification and scientists are working on plants with greater pest or disease resistance and greater health benefits. For better or worse, genetic modification is an issue we will need to confront at some time, whether we grow or buy tomatoes.

Tomatoes in the garden

Introduction

There is a huge range of tomato varieties available (thousands worldwide), from the tiny Matt's Wild Cherry to the giant Ponderosa, which weighs up to 1.5kg (3lb 2oz). Tomatoes are actually short-lived perennials, but they are best grown as annuals and there are varieties that will suit the vagaries of the British climate as well as those which will do well in the shelter of a greenhouse or polytunnel. Cool, damp summers can actually produce very good tomatoes. The sowing and planting times given in this book assume you are planting outside or have an unheated greenhouse. With a heated greenhouse, you can advance and extend the seasons considerably.

All tomatoes do well in containers, meaning that you can grow them literally anywhere, and many look very attractive. If you eat tomatoes immediately after picking them, their high levels of sugar will not have had a chance to turn into starch and they will taste much better than anything you can buy. Supermarket tomatoes are usually grown under glass, with their roots in water rather than soil, fed computer-controlled nutrients at preset intervals and encouraged to develop thick skins so they travel well. Even many 'vine-ripened' varieties are subjected to this regime. These methods produce high yields of uniform-looking fruits, but often at the expense of flavour.

The fruit that's a vegetable

Although tomatoes are grown and eaten as vegetables, in botanical terms they are actually fruits. The tomatoes themselves are berries, having developed from a fertilised ovary, but this makes little difference to the way we grow and eat them. Their Latin name, *Lycopersicon esculentum*, meaning 'edible wolf peach', clearly shows the confusion the plants caused – a bizarre mixture of the edible, gentle and dangerous. The wolf part of the name comes from the tomato's close links with belladonna, a plant used by witches in Germany to summon werewolves, and the peach part refers to the fact that the first tomatoes to reach Europe were orangey-yellow, resembling small peaches. The name was originally used by the Greek naturalist Galen to describe another plant 1,400 years ago, but the details of the plant have been lost and *Lycopersicon esculentum* is now very much the tomato.

Types of tomatoes

Most tomato plants are either cordons or bushes and it is important to know which you are growing, as they have different requirements. Both will give you a good crop of tomatoes and each has its pros and cons. One or two varieties can be trained as either, and some grow as semi-bushes (also known as semi-determinates) and are explained below.

Tomato plants are also divided by the type of fruit they produce, most falling into one of the following

categories: beefsteak, globe, cherry or plum. There is a
selection of recommended varieties on pages 48–53.

Cordons

Also known as indeterminates or vines, cordons are the
most common type of tomato. The plants will continue
growing until the first frosts and can easily reach up to
6m (20ft), with some commercial plants reaching 40m
(131ft), and even in Britain they will continue growing
and fruiting well into autumn. They are very good for
small spaces as the plants grow straight up and if they
are pinched out, do not spread much. Cordons are
perfect for growing in rows in a greenhouse or in the
garden, or on patios or balconies where you have
little ground space but lots of
headroom. If you grow them
in a greenhouse, you can
train them right up into
the roof and therefore
extend your harvest
considerably. They
flower and fruit over
a long period, avoiding
the problem of having
a glut, but do need
more regular tending
than bushes.

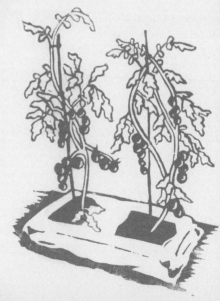

Bushes

These are also known as determinates and will grow to a set height and then stop. They bush out and have lots of side shoots, each of which bears flowers, and later fruits, at its tip. Most grow to about 1m (3ft), but this group also includes dwarf plants that can be grown in hanging baskets. The upright varieties may need support to stop the weight of the fruit pulling the stems down, but generally they require less day-to-day maintenance than cordons and will survive a certain amount of neglect. They are a better choice for poor soil or windy sites. The downsides are that all the fruit tends to ripen at once, and bushes take up more room than cordons.

Semi-bushes

Some cultivars grow in a similar way to bushes, but reach a greater height and produce a greater crop. These are known as semi-bushes or semi-determinants. They need support but do not need pinching out, although it is often worth removing some of the side shoots to restrict the size of the plant and improve the quality of the fruit.

Certain cultivars, such as Legend, can be grown as either a cordon or a bush. You can train the plant as a cordon or leave a couple of the lower shoots and it will spread out to form a large bush.

Beefsteak tomatoes

These are the giants of the tomato world. Many grow as bushes and all need long, hot summers for the tomatoes to ripen properly. Marmande is one of the varieties that will do well outside in British summers.

Globe tomatoes

Globe tomatoes are the most common type of tomato and, thanks to tasteless supermarket specimens, the ones with a reputation for being dull. The ones you grow at home will taste totally different. Most grow on cordons and many do well outside. They are all a similar shape, but come in a wide range of colours.

Cherry tomatoes

These little tomatoes are easy to grow outside as they ripen quickly. The smallest fruits are called 'currants', while the larger ones are described as 'cocktail'. Some grow as cordons and others as small bushes – these can be grown in small containers or allowed to tumble over the sides of hanging baskets.

Plum tomatoes

Not all plum tomatoes will ripen well outdoors in Britain, so choose the variety carefully. Any variety with a Royal Horticultural Society Award of Garden Merit (AGM) should be a safe bet. Cherry plums are baby plum tomatoes, most of which will do well inside or out.

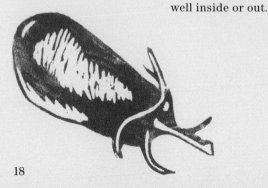

Growing outdoors and indoors

The decision whether to grow tomatoes out in the open or 'indoors' (in a greenhouse or polytunnel) will probably be down to the conditions and space in your garden. Most 'indoor' and 'outdoor' varieties will grow in either situation, but may not perform so well if not planted in the recommended location. Large tomatoes, in particular, need a long growing season and often do better with some protection. Plants grown indoors will give higher and more reliable yields, whereas those outdoors may produce fruit with a better flavour, especially if it is a good summer. In an ideal world you would grow a few of each.

Planting in the garden

Put the plants in a sheltered, sunny spot, ideally against a brick wall, which will absorb heat during the day and release it at night. The season is roughly a month shorter than for plants grown under cover, so grow small or early varieties that will ripen before the cold of autumn. If you are growing plants from seed, you will need to start them off with some protection, either in a heated propagator or on a warm window-sill. Once established, tomatoes are actually quite robust, standing up well to a bit of wind and rain, as long as they get plenty of sunshine in between.

Cold frames

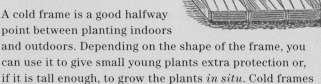

A cold frame is a good halfway
point between planting indoors
and outdoors. Depending on the shape of the frame, you
can use it to give small young plants extra protection or,
if it is tall enough, to grow the plants *in situ*. Cold frames
are very useful for toughening up indoor-grown seedlings
before they are planted outside.

Greenhouses and polytunnels

Greenhouses and polytunnels provide warmth, which
will extend the growing season and also provide a certain
amount of protection against blight. The extended season
will increase the range of tomatoes you can grow, making
plum tomatoes and large beefsteaks a practical option.
Most polytunnels consist of semicircular frames covered
with a tough polythene that lets 90 per cent of the light
through. Try to position a polytunnel along a north-south
axis, so one side doesn't get much hotter than the other.
Polytunnels are relatively cheap and as they are easy to
move, you can include them in your crop rotation system.
Against all these benefits, they can be hard to ventilate in
a hot summer, tend not to give you very much available
growing height, and look pretty hideous.

   A greenhouse, on the other hand, can be truly
beautiful as well as extremely useful. A tall greenhouse
will enable you to grow huge cordons; training them up
into the roof will produce a harvest of tomatoes right
through the autumn. You can put the plants directly in
the ground, or use pots or grow bags, but if you plant

directly in the soil you will need to completely replace it every three to four years to prevent nutritional depletion and diseases.

Outside, tomatoes are easily pollinated by insects and the wind; inside, you may need to help the plants by tapping the flowers. You may also need to mist the plants and protect them from the midday sun if it is very hot. Finally, you need to keep the glass or plastic very clean. Tomatoes need good levels of light to do well.

Varieties for outdoors

Britain's Breakfast, Glacier, Marmande, San Marzano, Scotland Yellow, Siberian, Sub-Arctic Plenty, most cherry tomatoes.

Varieties for indoors

Shirley F1, Sun Belle, most beefsteak tomatoes.

Varieties for indoors or outdoors

Ailsa Craig, Alicante, Ferline F1, Ildi, Myriade F1, Olivade F1, Stupice, Tigerella, Yellow Pear.

Site and soil

Above all, tomatoes need sunshine. Even the shade of
the foliage itself can reduce the flavour of the fruits.
Try to position them against a sunny wall: the brick will
absorb heat during the day and release it at night, giving
the tomatoes the constant temperature that they like.
Tomatoes like a well-drained, moisture-retentive soil
with a pH of 5.5-7 (6-6.5 is ideal). If the soil is too rich
or has too much nitrogen, the plants will grow leaves at
the expense of flowers and fruits. Ideally, you should dig
in compost or well-rotted manure in the autumn and
leave it to break down over the winter.

Crop rotation

Practising crop rotation has the double benefit of
reducing the risk of disease and ensuring that the soil
does not become exhausted. Roots will break up the
soil, ready for legumes the following year, which will
leave nitrogen in the soil, which can then be used for
brassicas the year after. Tomatoes are from the same
family as potatoes, but can be planted either within the
root or the legume group. Plant them as far away from
potatoes as possible (to minimise the risk of blight) and
in a sunny and sheltered spot. By growing your
vegetables in this way, you will actually replenish the
nutrients in the soil over the years, rather than exhaust
them. It will be extremely unlikely that you will be able
to carry out a perfect rotation system, particularly if
you grow vegetables in amongst flowers and other
ornamentals, but any movement is better than none.

Seeds or plants?

You can either grow tomatoes from seed or buy small plants. Tomatoes are simple to grow from seed, germinating easily, and this is the method to use if you want a lot of tomato plants (it works out much cheaper) or if you want to grow unusual varieties. Many heritage varieties cannot be sold because they fall foul of EU regulations, but gardening clubs and organisations such as Garden Organic can give them away to members and this is a good way to obtain some rare and interesting varieties. If you are short of space and only have room for three or four tomato plants, it is probably easier to buy plants and get a selection of different varieties. Growing tomatoes from seed takes up a certain amount of space and is not really practical if you only want one plant of each variety.

Plants should be ready to buy in mid- to late spring. Choose plants that look sturdy – height isn't necessary at this stage. You may also like to consider buying plants by mail order: these usually come in small plugs and should be potted on into slightly larger pots straight away. Be careful not to over-water young plants: the soil should be damp but not soggy.

Some suppliers are now selling grafted plants. These were originally used by commercial growers and are useful as they establish themselves quickly in the soil and crop earlier than plants grown from seed. The top growth of a tomato seedling is spliced onto a rootstock bred from a wild species, usually *Solanum pimpinelifolium*. This rootstock does not mind low temperatures or poor soil and has a good resistance to root diseases.

Sowing seeds

The time to sow is mid- to late spring. There is no point in sowing any earlier as the weather will not be warm enough by the time the plants are ready to flower. You can sow the seeds of cordon tomatoes all at once, but stagger the sowing of bush tomatoes so your tomatoes don't all ripen together. Plant the seeds in trays, small pots or individual modules in trays. Fill the containers with general-purpose peat-free compost or seed compost, water and leave to drain. Seed compost drains well but has very few nutrients, so you will need to re-pot the plants as soon as they start to grow.

Sprinkle the seeds on top of the compost and cover lightly with sieved compost or vermiculite (a mineral used to aid germination). Tomato seeds are fairly large and easy to handle, so spread them out as this will make potting on much easier. Allow six to eight seeds to an 8–10cm (3–4in) pot, or two per module.

Germination

Tomatoes germinate best between 15°C (59°F) and 20°C (68°F). You can put the containers on a warm window-sill or, ideally, a heated propagating mat. Do not allow the compost to dry out. Cover the seeds so they are in darkness and move them into the light as soon as they germinate. Tomatoes germinate extremely easily; even seeds from tinned tomatoes will grow into plants, although it is not usually worth growing these varieties in Britain as they require too much warmth.

Within eight to sixteen days, the plants should begin to appear. Keep an eye on the pots, as some varieties can be as quick as four days, whereas others may take up to 21 days. The plants need to be kept somewhere light and well ventilated, but the temperature can now be reduced to 10–15°C (50–59°F).

Potting on and hardening off

Once the plants grow true leaves (rather than the first pair, which is 'false'), you will be able to see which plants are the healthiest. Discard the weakest ones so you end up with three to four plants to a pot or one plant per module. Once the plants start to fill out, you need to pot them on into a slightly larger pot. If you planted the seeds in seed compost, you will need to do this as soon as the true leaves appear, as seed compost does not have sufficient nutrients to support growing plants. Increase the pot size and depth gradually: if you put plants directly into a large pot, their roots will grow straight out, leaving a gap at the centre of the root system, whereas you want to encourage the roots to grow strongly and evenly throughout the pot. A certain amount of restriction of the roots encourages more flowers and fruit. Once the plants are in 9cm (3½in)

pots, you can leave them until they begin to develop flowers, at which point they are ready to move to their final position.

If you are going to plant the tomatoes outside, you will need to harden them off before exposing them to the elements. The stems and foliage of plants growing in a sheltered environment tend to be delicate and can easily be damaged by low temperatures or wind. Put the plants outside on warm days, gradually increasing the amount of time they spend outside by a few hours until they are robust enough to stay out all night. Move the plants to somewhere sheltered at night, but do not bring them back inside as they will never toughen up. If you have a cold frame, put the plants in it, leaving the top open on sunny days and closed on wet or windy days and at night. Cut-off clear plastic bottles make good cloches for young plants. The speed at which the plants acclimatise will depend, to a certain extent, on the weather, but plants that are hardened off slowly over a couple of weeks usually do best.

Getting a second crop

If you have a warm or heated greenhouse, you can grow a second crop which will give you fresh tomatoes in winter and possibly even on Christmas Day. Cordons will continue growing and cropping as long as there is sufficient warmth, but the plants can get very long and straggly and a neater alternative is to sow a second batch of seeds in late spring or even early summer. These tomatoes will grow through the summer and begin to crop just as the first batch is finishing.

An alternative method is to take cuttings from existing cordons in midsummer. Allow one of the side shoots to grow until it is about 13cm (5in) long and then cut it away cleanly. Stand it in water, and within a couple of weeks the stem should develop roots. Once these look reasonably sturdy, the cutting can be planted in a small pot of compost. Re-plant in a larger container as soon as the flowers appear. Keep in a warm greenhouse for a Christmas crop.

Planting

Timing

Tomatoes cannot be planted outside until all risk of frost has passed, the air temperature is at least 7°C (45°F) and the soil temperature is 10°C (50°F). In practical terms, this means early summer, not late spring. It is not enough to wait for warm days – you have to wait for reasonably warm nights too, as tomatoes do not like great fluctuations in temperature.

Spacing

Tomatoes need to be planted sufficiently far apart to allow the air to circulate around the plant and so that you can easily reach all sides to pick the fruit. Cordons in a greenhouse need a bit more space than those outside, as they will be growing for a longer time.

Bushes Allow 60cm–1m (2ft–3ft) between each plant and 2m (6ft) between rows.
Cordons in a greenhouse Allow 45cm (18in) between each plant and 1m (3ft) between rows.
Cordons outdoors Allow 38–45cm (15–18in) between plants.
Dwarf varieties Allow 23–30cm (9–12in) between plants, depending on the variety.

Support

Put the support in place before you put the plants into the soil, to avoid damaging the roots. It is worth taking into consideration the fact that much of the support will be on show while the tomato is growing up it. Coloured stakes, spirals, tripods and wigwams can all look attractive in their own right, depending on the style of your garden.

Cordons growing outside will need a strong stake, as the plants will be laden with heavy fruit. Cordons grown in a greenhouse can reach a much greater height and the best method of support is to create a framework of strings or wires coming down from the roof. Either tie the string to the base of the plant or start the plant off to grow up a cane and tie the string to that. If you intend to grow a lot of tomatoes, it is worth fixing heavy-duty galvanised wire horizontally at 60cm (2ft) intervals, so you can attach the vertical canes or strings to that.

Bushes will usually stand up on their own, but the weight of the tomatoes can pull them down. You can either fix a circle of wire mesh around the plant – 30cm (1ft) tall and 45cm (18in) across – or surround the plant with low stakes and tie the stems to these.

Planting depth

Make sure that the soil and plant are both damp but not waterlogged. Bury the plant up to the first set of leaves and then gently firm it in. Planting at this depth will encourage the plant to grow more roots, which will anchor it firmly and enable it to take up more moisture and nutrients.

Planting in straw bales

Straw is easy for a tomato plant's roots to grow in, it holds moisture well and it will also provide you with quantities of organic matter at the end of the season. Use organic straw so there are no potentially harmful chemicals, and two to three weeks before planting, water well and add a nitrogen feed so the straw starts to decompose. This will soften and warm the straw, making it attractive for the tomato plant's roots. Wrapping the bale in plastic will retain water and warmth, but the straw can get too hot in summer and while a straw bale looks rustic and attractive, a heap of decomposing straw wrapped in plastic looks ugly. Plant the tomatoes in a mound of potting compost on the surface of the bale and water and feed as you would for container plants, but in smaller quantities. At the end of the season, you can compost the straw or dig it straight into the soil.

Planting upside down

You can grow tomatoes upside down in a specially designed bag of compost that is hung from a pole or wall. In theory the plant grows better this way (with its roots warmed by the sun) and produces larger yields and bigger tomatoes as the nutrients are pulled down by gravity.

Care

Tomatoes are not nearly as delicate as you might imagine and the best tomatoes often come from the scruffiest-looking plants; slightly starved plants tend to produce more intensely flavoured fruit.

Mulching

Wherever you grow tomatoes, a layer of mulch will help them enormously. Chopped-up comfrey leaves are a good choice – they reduce water loss through evaporation and feed the plants as they rot down. Lay down a 5cm (2in) layer of comfrey leaves when you put the plants in the ground, leaving a gap around each stem so the mulch won't cause it to rot. Mulch will also stop weeds growing up and competing with the tomatoes. If you do need to weed, do it gently, taking care not to damage the stems of the tomatoes.

Feeding

Outdoor tomatoes grown in well-prepared soil should not really need feeding, but all tomatoes grown in containers need regular supplements. The nutrients in multipurpose compost and even grow bags do not last more than about three to four weeks, and after that the plant will be dependent on you for its nutrients. It is important to supply the correct nutrients in the correct quantities: too much can do as much harm as too little.

Starting about a month after you have planted them, give tomatoes in containers a liquid feed every week.

You can use a specialist tomato food, liquid seaweed or prepare your own food, but the important thing is to give the plants the correct balance. Nitrogen (N) will encourage leafy growth, phosphorous (P) will give the plant strong roots, and potassium or potash (K) will increase the production of flowers and fruit, so choose a food with high levels of potash for lots of fruits. Potash also toughens the stems and leaves, making them less vulnerable to attack.

One of the best foods for tomatoes is home-made liquid comfrey. The comfrey variety Bocking 14 is non-invasive and once the plant is established, in its second year onwards, you can cut it down to the ground three times a year and use the leaves for mulch or food.

Tear the comfrey leaves and fill a lidded bucket (the lid is important – the mixture stinks), add water so the leaves are submerged, put the lid on and leave it. You will be able to tell when it is ready because it will smell strongly – probably in about two to three weeks' time. The strength of the liquid will depend on how tightly you packed the leaves, but if you now dilute it 1:5 with water this will probably make it the right consistency. Siphon the liquid into a plastic bottle to save as the feed and put the leaves on the compost heap, but have another layer of something ready to put on top – it is impossible to over-emphasise how awful the smell is. If you choose to leave the liquid in the bucket with the leaves, increase the ratio of water because the mixture will get stronger with each successive week.

Watering

Tomatoes need water, but if you give them too much it can make the fruit large and tasteless. Provide a constant supply of water: erratic watering will stress the plants and can cause problems. As a general rule, plants in open soil should be watered every three to four days, and those in containers every day. Once the fruits start to form, this should be reduced so that the soil remains just moist. In very hot weather, use tepid water to avoid stressing the plant.

To ensure that the roots get a good supply of water, you could bury a flowerpot in the ground near the plant and fill that with water, which will then drain directly to the roots. You can also use a ring pot (see page 37).

Tying in

As a cordon grows you will need to tie it to its support. Tie the stems in place with soft garden twine, allowing for the extra weight that will come from the fruits. At the same time you can also remove any lower leaves that have turned yellow or any that are shading ripening fruit. Bushes can be kept upright with a simple circular support surrounding them.

Pinching out

Tomatoes grow three different shoots out of the main stem: flowering, leafy and branching. The flowering shoots produce the tomato harvest. The stems with leaves can be left until they turn yellow, at which point they can be removed, increasing the air circulation.

The branching shoots are potential side branches, which grow in the angle between the main stem and the leafy stems. These only appear on cordons and should be removed when they are little. When they are small you can simply pinch them off, but if they are larger it is better to cut them off so you don't damage the main stem. These side shoots will produce tomatoes, but sap a huge amount of energy from the plant and only produce small fruits. If you miss some it doesn't matter too much: there is a school of thought that says you shouldn't pinch out side shoots at all so the plant doesn't develop vulnerable points.

You should also pinch out the tip of a cordon when it has reached the required height. In a warm greenhouse you can let cordons go on growing until they stop naturally, but outdoors there is not much point letting the plant grow beyond having five or six trusses (flower heads that will grow into tomatoes).

If you want to create a double cordon with two stems, you should allow the bottom side shoot to grow up and form a second stem. As long as the plant receives sufficient sun, water and nutrients, you will be able to harvest twice the number of tomatoes. This is a useful method if you have a conservatory with lots of roof space but don't want too many pots at ground level.

Tomatoes as ornamentals

Tomato plants are just as at home in the middle of
a flower bed as they are in a rotated vegetable plan.
Depending on which variety you choose they can be tall
and stately, short and bushy or planted to tumble over
the edge of a container. The flowers are small but the
tomatoes themselves look striking, even while they are
ripening. Cherry tomatoes, in particular, can grow long
strings of fruits which remain on the plant over an
extended period.

Tomatoes go particularly well with late-flowering
plants such as sunflowers, Michaelmas daisies,
chrysanthemums and cosmos. The foliage of these will
also disguise the stems of the tomato plants when they
get bare and leggy. Don't put the plants so close that
they surround the tomato, but stagger them so the sun
can still get through to reach the fruit. Low plants such
as marigolds and snapdragons can go in front and
nasturtiums can be allowed to climb up the tomatoes
(they will do no harm).

Small bush tomatoes
can be used in hanging
baskets and also in
window boxes or to
edge raised beds.
They go particularly
well with lobelia
(*L. erinus*), poached egg
plant (*Limnanthes
douglasii*) and nasturtiums
(*Tropaeolum majus*).

Growing tomatoes in containers

Tomatoes grow brilliantly well in containers and actually produce more fruit if their roots are slightly constricted. The other great advantage of containers is that you can move them, putting the plants indoors or outdoors as the weather dictates and placing the tomatoes in a prominent position when they are looking their best. All types do well in containers, but cherry tomatoes are best for small containers.

The minimum size of pot for successfully growing tomatoes is 25–30cm (10–12in) in diameter, although a pot that is a bit bigger is better. Grow bags, or an equivalent-sized trough, will support three plants. Pots with a depth of 45cm (18in) are best, as they will retain more water. Tomatoes will grow in pots or troughs that are only 20cm (8in) deep, but you will need to water them more regularly.

Grow bags

Grow bags are the most common way to grow tomatoes in containers and the most unattractive. You wouldn't leave a large plastic bag lying in the middle of your garden, so why deliberately plant one up? They have their use in a vegetable garden or greenhouse, as it means that you can grow tomatoes in the same optimum position year after year without depleting the soil, but in all situations it looks better if you decant the compost from the grow bag into some sort of attractive container.

If you are using a grow bag, you need to plant it *in situ*, as they are impossible to move with plants in them. First, pummel the bag a bit to break up the compost, because it can become very compacted if stored for any length of time. Then make sure there are plenty of drainage holes. These are often marked on the bottom, but there aren't usually enough – you want a hole about every 15cm (6in). Cut individual holes in which to insert the plants, making them large enough to allow you to water the plants but small enough to prevent the compost spilling out.

Pots and ring pots

One of the best ways to use a grow bag is to combine it with a pot. You can cut the bottom out of a largish pot or, better still, use a ring pot and sink it into the grow bag. This will give the roots more space to spread and retain water efficiently. The added height of the compost will also hold the supporting cane in place more firmly. Ring pots consist of an ordinary plastic pot surrounded by an outer ring or reservoir for water. You fill the outer ring and the water gradually seeps down into the soil, giving the plants a constant supply.

Large pots are a more attractive option and you can use anything, as long as it has drainage. Put a layer of gravel in the bottom and then fill with compost. Either use the contents of a grow bag, peat-free multipurpose potting compost, or a 50:50 mixture of John Innes No. 2 and peat-free multipurpose potting compost. Do not be tempted to reuse old compost: not only will the nutrients have been used up but the structure will have broken down and you run the risk of passing on disease.

Hanging baskets

Hanging baskets can be used for dwarf bush varieties, which will tumble attractively over the sides. One plant will fit in a small basket with a diameter of 25cm (10in), or put three plants in a larger one. Larger baskets will retain water more efficiently, which is an important consideration; if your basket is in a sunny spot, you will need to water twice a day to stop it drying out. Use a loam-based compost mixed with perlite or vermiculite to lessen the weight, and add water-retaining granules to help drainage. Avoid John Innes compost, as it is too heavy. Good trailing tomato varieties include Tumbler, Tumbling Tom Red and Tumbling Tom Yellow.

Companion planting

It is better to grow tomatoes mixed in with other plants as this moves away from monoculture and its attendant pitfalls. Growing single crops depletes the soil of its nutrients and increases the risk of pests and diseases, whereas a mixture of plants creates a healthy balance. All flowers go well with tomatoes and many will encourage bees and other beneficial insects, and there are only a few fruits and vegetables you should avoid.

The tomato guest list

Good companions

Marigolds (*Tagetes*) – their roots benefit tomatoes and they deter whitefly and aphids.
Chives and **alliums** deter aphids, slugs and snails.
Basil improves flavour and deters thrips (thunderflies).
Oregano deters aphids and many other pests.
Nettles encourage the fruits to ripen (but these are probably not plants you will want in your garden).
Borage deters moths.

Bad companions

Dill
Fennel
Kohlrabi
Potatoes
Rosemary
Strawberries

Problems

Many problems can be avoided if you grow the plants
in a healthy environment. Make sure there is a good air
flow around the plants, especially under cover, avoid
having too much nitrogen in the soil as this encourages
soft, vulnerable growth, and provide plenty of potash
(comfrey contains high levels) to strengthen the stems
and leaves. Water correctly so that the plant is never
stressed. Companion planting will deter many pests.
Finally, practise crop rotation as far as your plot allows.

Blight

Blight is the worst thing that can happen to tomatoes –
within days they will go from healthy plants to
blackened wrecks. It is most common towards the end
of hot, wet summers. Pale brown patches appear on the
leaves and rapidly spread over the whole plant. You can
sometimes save the plants if you remove the leaves and
spray with Bordeaux mixture (this is organically
allowed but isn't good for the overall health of the
garden), but you will probably have to dig them up and
destroy them. The spores overwinter in infected
material and although in theory a compost heap should
generate enough heat to destroy them, it seems safer to
burn the plants or bag them and throw away.

Never plant tomatoes near potatoes, as both are
susceptible and will pass it between each other. Leave
a gap of at least two years between growing tomatoes in
the same area of soil. Growing plants indoors offers
some protection.

Wilt

Fusarium and *Verticillium* wilt cause the plants to droop during the day, although they usually recover at night. Prevention is the best action: do not put plants out when it is still cold, rotate your crops and plant seedlings deeply so they grow strong roots.

Botrytis or mould

Botrytis can cause the stems to develop fluffy grey patches, the flowers to turn grey and the fruits to develop translucent or ghost spots. It is most common in greenhouses and polytunnels, and can be prevented by providing ventilation and avoiding high humidity levels.

Viruses

Viruses can cause mottled, misshapen leaves and stunted plants. You may still get a reasonable crop and you can't do much about it once your plants are affected. Destroy the plants and sterilise tools at the end of the season.

Blossom end rot

Blossom end rot causes a hard brown patch to appear at the end of the fruit, usually when the plant is stressed and does not take up sufficient calcium. It can be prevented by regular watering and mist-spraying plants under glass in hot weather. It tends to affect indoor plants and is most common on very acidic soil. Small-fruited varieties are usually less susceptible.

Split fruits

This is usually caused by an erratic water supply or a sudden burst of growth if sunny weather follows an overcast period. Tomatoes become more vulnerable as they ripen, because their skins become thinner. The fruits are fine to eat, but need to be used immediately as they will not keep.

Greenback

Greenback, or whitewall, causes hard green patches to appear at the top of the fruit. It is most common under glass and is due to overheating and sun-scorch. You can usually prevent it by ensuring adequate shade and ventilation, and a regular water supply. Most of the latest varieties are not susceptible to it.

Leaf curl

When the leaves curl up lengthways, it is not fatal, but it does not help the overall health of the plant. It can be caused by irregular water supplies, but is most common in greenhouses with large variations between daytime and night-time temperatures. Shade the plants from the midday sun, leave the greenhouse doors open during the day and then close them before it cools in the evening.

Slugs and snails

Young plants are most at risk from slugs and snails. Surround each plant with coffee grounds or grit, or create a barrier around containers using copper tape.

Whitefly and aphids

The adults lay eggs on the lower leaves and the little pests that hatch eat the leaves, suck the sap and excrete honeydew – where fungus may grow. They are most common in greenhouses, where they overwinter on perennials such as fuchsias. Basil and French marigolds (*Tagetes minuta*) are good deterrents, as are biological control wasps: use *Encarsia formosa* against whitefly and *Aphidius colemani* against aphids.

Red spider mite

Red spider mites make tomato leaves appear dry and cover them with tiny holes. They are most common in warm, dry greenhouses. They are actually green and only turn red when they are getting ready to hibernate. Small infestations can be dealt with by spraying the plants with water; for more serious attacks, use the biological control *Phytosiulus persimilis*. Clear the area of all foliage in autumn, so the mites do not have anywhere to hibernate.

Tomato moth caterpillar

The tomato moth caterpillar is 4cm (1½in) long and greenish-brown with a yellow stripe along its body. It hatches in late spring and early summer and will munch its way through your fruit. It is quite easy to spot the eggs on the undersides of the leaves: simply remove them before they hatch.

Harvesting

Bush tomatoes should be ready to harvest within seven to eight weeks and those on cordons within ten to twelve weeks. Pick the fruits as they ripen, so the plant can concentrate on new ones. Indoor tomatoes will go on ripening throughout the autumn, but those growing outdoors are unlikely to ripen after September as the days are too short and the nights too cold.

To ripen green tomatoes, you can either cut the entire cordon and hang it upside down in a frost-free shed, or ripen the fruits individually. Pick them with the calyx (the spiky green crown) and put them in a drawer or paper bag with an apple or banana. The tomatoes will ripen, but they will not have the flavour of those ripened in the sun. In many ways, it is better to accept that the season is over until next year. With luck you will have plenty of tomatoes stored, or frozen as sauce or chutney, and these will have more flavour than a few sad specimens from the tail end of the season.

Saving seeds

It is very easy to save tomato seeds and it is a good and cheap way of repeating a successful crop. Choose ripe fruits, wash the pulp off the seeds in a sieve and spread out the seeds on kitchen paper to dry. Once they are dry, leave them on the kitchen paper and store them in a paper bag in the fridge ready for the following spring. Note that seeds from F1 hybrids may be sterile or, if they do germinate, are unlikely to come true. Seeds from heirloom plants and some hybrids should come true.

THE
TWO MOST POPULAR AND
PROFITABLE
NOVELTIES
OF THE
YEAR

NEW DAVIS'S KIDNEY WAX BEANS

NEW IMPERIAL TOMATO

ONE PACKET OF EACH FOR 25 CENTS

Wᵐ HENRY MAULE,
PHILADELPHIA, U.S.A.

Varieties

CARTER'S GREEN GAGE TOMATO

It is important to grow a variety that will do well in the conditions you have – most beefsteaks grow better indoors in Britain, cherry tomatoes are the best for small containers, and many plum tomatoes need a long summer to ripen fully. As a general rule, the larger the tomato, the more sun (or at least warmth) it will need, whereas dwarf varieties tend to need less heat and ripen more quickly. Some tomatoes are bred to be grown indoors, others are designed for outdoors, and while a few will perform well in any situation, most do better given their chosen conditions. In the selection on pages 48–53, the plant's preference is listed first.

Flavour and colour

Taste is obviously an important consideration and here it is worth remembering that a supermarket variety will almost certainly taste better if you grow it yourself instead; most tomatoes lose something if subjected to mass-market growing techniques. Looks are also worth taking into account: some spectacular-looking tomatoes can be disappointing, but green ones, in particular, are often intensely flavoured. From red to yellow to bright green with shades of pink and even dark crimson, not to mention stripes and patches, the colour choices are almost limitless.

Hybrids and heirlooms

Many new varieties have disease resistance bred into them, but equally, many old varieties are naturally robust. An F1 hybrid results from the crossing of two pure-bred plants and may have advantages such as disease resistance or drought tolerance, while an ordinary hybrid is a modern variety that comes from the simple crossing of two distinct parents. F1 hybrids are expensive but give reliable results. Heritage or heirloom tomatoes tend to be older varieties, but there is no exact definition. Varieties with an Award of Garden Merit (AGM) from the RHS are always a good choice. These awards appear on the plant's label as a trophy symbol or the letters 'AGM'.

Deciding what to grow

Growing a mixture of a few favourites and one or two experiments will ensure that you get a crop of fruit you like, as well as possibly finding new ones to add to your list. The selection given on pages 48–53 includes a mixture of beef, cherry, globe and plum tomatoes, and cordons, bushes, F1 hybrids and heirlooms. The tomato's origin is given if it affects its growing conditions, and heirlooms and F1 varieties are indicated.

Strictly speaking, each different tomato is a cultivar, i.e. a cultivated variety. Tomatoes are usually referred to by their cultivar name rather than the Latin, e.g. Sungold, Tornado. Botanically these should be written within single inverted commas, but these are frequently omitted for ease of reading, as we have done in this book.

Tomato varieties

Beefsteak tomatoes

Black Krim/Black Crimea/Czerno Krimski
Cordon. Indoors or outdoors.
Heirloom from the Isle of Krim in the Black Sea. The fruit is deep red with green tints, sometimes appearing almost black. The plants are tolerant of reasonably low light and temperature levels, have good disease resistance and some blight resistance. Black Krim and Black Crimea are different cultivars, but they are very similar and frequently interchanged in catalogues.

Black Russian
Cordon. Indoors or outdoors.
Heirloom from Russia, originally grown by Capuchin monks. The fruits are deep purple, almost black, with dark flesh. Water carefully as they can be prone to splitting.

Brandywine
Cordon. Indoors; needs a hot summer outdoors.
Heirloom variety from America producing huge, deeply fissured fruits. Brandywine is pinkish-red, but red and yellow varieties are also available.

Burpee Delicious
Cordon. Indoors or outdoors.
An American variety producing big, round, juicy fruits. Overall yields, however, can be poor.

Caspian Pink
Cordon. Indoors.
This comes from the area around the Black Sea and although the winters there are very cold, the summers are hot, so they won't ripen well outside in Britain. The pink fruits are huge.

Costoluto Fiorentino
Cordon. Good grown outdoors, but need a long, hot summer. Otherwise they are fine indoors.
Heirloom from Italy. The medium-sized fruits are ribbed and juicy. Costoluto Genovese is similar, but more deeply ribbed.

Cuor di Bue
Cordon. Indoors.
Heirloom from Italy. The plants need lots of support, as the stems tend to be floppy and the fruits large. The fruits have firm flesh and few seeds.

Dombito
Cordon. Indoors or outdoors.
This grows into a fairly compact plant. The fruits ripen early and are large and round, with few seeds.

Legend
Cordon or bush. Outdoors or indoors.
This variety was bred in Oregon, where blight is a serious problem, and it has partial resistance to it. The flattish red fruits ripen very early and have very few seeds.

Marmande
Semi-bush. Outdoors in a warm spot.
Heirloom variety from France. The large, irregularly shaped, deep red fruits ripen reliably. Super Marmande crops earlier and has better disease resistance, especially against wilt.

Purple Calabash
Cordon. Indoors or outdoors in a very sheltered spot.
Heirloom from America. These tomatoes are deeply fissured, weirdly shaped and a rich chocolate-brown colour. The plants do well on poor soil and do not mind partial shade, but the best flavour comes when grown in full sun.

Globe tomatoes

Ailsa Craig
Cordon. Outdoors or indoors.
Heirloom bred in Scotland. These plants produce high yields of bright red tomatoes which ripen reliably outside.

Alicante
Cordon. Outdoors or indoors.
Heirloom, bred in England. These plants produce reliably high yields even in poor summers.

Ferline F1
Cordon. Outdoors or indoors.
F1 hybrid, bred in France. The deep red tomatoes are large, with solid flesh, and ripen very early. The plant has some resistance to blight and good resistance to wilt.

Glacier
Semi-bush. Outdoors.
Bred in Sweden, this variety is very tolerant of cold weather and will produce a good crop even in cool summers.

Green Zebra
Cordon. Indoors or outdoors in a warm spot.
An heirloom from America with fruits that have amazing dark green stripes on a yellowy-green skin. They need to be picked before an orange tinge appears.

Harbinger
Cordon. Outdoors or indoors.
Heirloom. This variety does not mind cool summers and crops over a long period. The

fruits have thin skins and can be various sizes.

Scotland Yellow
Cordon. Outdoors or indoors.
This was bred in Scotland to tolerate cool summers, and produces attractive buttery-yellow fruits.

Shirley F1
Cordon. Best indoors.
The compact plants give high yields of medium-sized fruits and are resistant to leaf mould, wilt and most viruses. For the best-flavoured fruit, feed the plants regularly with potash (comfrey).

Siberian
Bush. Outdoors.
This heirloom from Russia crops early and will tolerate cold temperatures. The tomatoes are bright red.

Stupice
Cordon. Indoors or outdoors.
This heirloom variety from Czechoslovakia ripens very early and gives high yields. The plant stops naturally at about 1.2–1.5m (4–5ft), is tolerant of cold and is partially resistant to blight.

Sub-Arctic Plenty
Dwarf bush. Outdoors.
The plant was bred specifically to produce good fruits in cool, short summers for the US Air Force troops who were stationed in Greenland. The plant fruits in a very short time and will set fruit even in cold weather. Plant a late sowing for harvesting in autumn. Also available: Sub-Arctic Maxi.

Tigerella
Cordon. Outdoors or indoors.
Heirloom, bred in England. Sometimes called Mr Stripey – the tomatoes are dark red with greenish-yellow and orange stripes. It is a robust plant with high yields that ripen early.

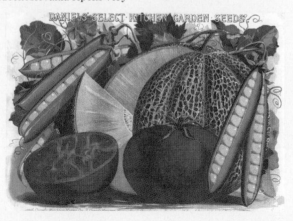

DANIELS' SELECT KITCHEN GARDEN SEEDS

Cherry tomatoes

Black Cherry
Cordon. Outdoors or indoors.
Heirloom from America. The dark fruits are small and sweet and look exactly like cherries. The plants reliably produce high yields.

Brown Berry/Chocodel
Cordon. Outdoors or indoors.
The tomatoes are a deep, chocolatey red with green flesh and a smoky taste. Brown Berry and Chocodel are actually different varieties, but are often linked together in catalogues.

Favorita F1
Cordon. Indoors or outdoors.
These large plants give high yields of little tomatoes on long trusses. They become sweeter in a hot summer but are tolerant of wet weather.

Gardener's Delight
Cordon. Indoors or outdoors.
Heirloom. These large cherry tomatoes are bright red and easy to grow. There is a Del series of fruits in various colours: Chocodel (brown), Striadel (red), Daffodel (yellow), Rosadel (pink) and Albadel (creamy yellow).

Koralik
Bush. Indoors or outdoors.
This forms a sprawling bush with masses of tiny tomatoes. It crops very early and has some blight resistance.

Matt's Wild Cherry
Cordon. Outdoors.
This originated in Mexico and has partial blight resistance. The tiny fruits are like little currants.

Moneymaker
Cordon. Indoors or outdoors.
Heirloom. Ubiquitous in the 1960s and can be dull, but very reliable.

Quentin
Cordon/bush. Outdoors or indoors.
This was bred in England to provide a long season under glass, but does very well outside.

Red Alert
Bush. Outdoors or indoors.
This dwarf variety tumbles well out of hanging baskets and window boxes. It ripens very early, producing sweet, oval-shaped fruits.

Sungold F1
Cordon. Indoors or outdoors.
F1 hybrid bred in Japan. These small, orangey-yellow tomatoes are one of the sweetest varieties. They ripen easily and crop over a long period.

Sweet Million F1
Cordon. Indoors or outdoors.
F1 hybrid. This grows into a very vigorous plant with good virus resistance. It produces long strings of tiny red tomatoes.

Tornado
Bush. Outdoors.
This produces large cherry fruits and gives a good yield even in poor summers. The plants do well in containers.

Tumbler
Bush. Outdoors or indoors.
This is an easy dwarf plant, which is excellent in containers or hanging baskets. It is the best choice for very small spaces.

Tumbling Tom Red
Bush. Outdoors or indoors.
These sweet tomatoes are perfect for hanging baskets. They are tolerant of poor weather. Tumbling Tom Yellow is similar to Tumbling Tom Red but less vigorous and not as sweet. The two look good grown together.

Lycopersicon pimpinellifolium
Bush. Indoors or outdoors.
This is one of the original wild tomatoes from South America. The plant is bushy and sprawling, and produces tiny, currant-like fruits. It looks good tied loosely along a trellis.

Plum tomatoes

Britain's Breakfast
Cordon. Outdoors or indoors.
The red, lemon-shaped fruits grow on huge trusses, holding up to 60 fruits.

Dasher
Cordon. Indoors or outdoors.
These mini plums have long, attractive trusses.

Floridity F1
Cordon. Indoors or outdoors.
F1 hybrid bred in England. This has a long cropping season. The bright red cherry plums came top in an RHS taste trial.

Ildi
Cordon. Indoors or outdoors.
Bred in Germany. The plant grows high yields of yellow cherry plums in long strings. The fruits have a good resistance to splitting.

Myriade F1
Cordon. Indoors or outdoors.
These are vigorous plants with long trusses of large fruits.

Olivade F1
Cordon. Indoors or outdoors.
This gives high yields of large fruits with dark, juicy flesh. It has good resistance to wilt and viruses.

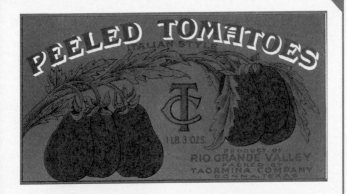

Principe Borghese
Cordon. Outdoors in a warm spot.
Heirloom from Italy. This needs good, well-composted soil and will then reward you with high yields.

Purple Russian
Cordon. Outdoors or indoors.
Heirloom bred in Russia. This is hardier than most plums, and the fruits are medium-sized and a deep maroon colour.

Roma
Bush. Indoors or outdoors.
Heirloom from America, despite its Italian-sounding name. The compact plant produces fruits with thick, juicy flesh and few seeds. They are best cooked, as the skin is quite thick. Roma VF is an improved variety with good resistance to wilt.

San Marzano
Cordon. Outdoors or indoors.
Heirloom from Italy. Crops well, with tomatoes that are larger than Roma and are especially tasty in sunny summers. There are many variants with improved characteristics or varied shapes; some are F1 hybrids, others come true from seed.

Sun Belle
Cordon. Indoors.
This will produce large numbers of small golden fruits, but needs the protection of glass to do well.

Yellow Pear
Cordon. Outdoors or indoors.
Heirloom. Not strictly a plum variety as the small, yellow fruits are pear-shaped. Dates from the seventeenth century and is very easy to grow, cropping over a long season.

Tomatoes in the kitchen

Making a choice

There is a huge range of tomatoes, from tiny round fruits like marbles to giant gnarled ones the size of a fist. As for colour, red is the first colour that springs to mind, but you can also get tomatoes that are yellow, orange, deep reddish-brown or stripy. There are even varieties that remain bright green when fully ripe. Many dishes benefit from a mixture of tomatoes: a few tiny yellow tomatoes scattered amongst wagon-wheel tomatoes in a tart will improve both the look and taste. Certain tomatoes are better for certain techniques, and some hold together better than others when cooked.

Cherry tomatoes

These are the smallest tomatoes and are usually the sweetest. They are very good raw (especially picked straight off the plant on a hot summer's day), but they can also be made into quick, fresh-tasting sauces. You can grill and fry them, or roast them either individually or on the vine.

Globe tomatoes

These are the common supermarket tomatoes, but they vary widely and some are really delicious. Good ones can be sliced in salads, and if you find you have dull tomatoes, either roast them or make them into a slow-cooked sauce, to give them a little more flavour.

Beefsteak tomatoes

Spectacular as they may look, giant tomatoes can sometimes be a bit tasteless. Use the pick of the crop for salads and the others for stuffing. They are very useful for sandwiches, as their beefy flesh does not make the bread go soggy.

Plum tomatoes

These are an excellent choice for cooking. They have firm flesh that doesn't disintegrate, fewer seeds and thick skins that peel away easily. Cooking also intensifies their flavour. Be sure to use well-ripened tomatoes for the best results. Plum tomatoes can also be eaten raw.

Cherry plum tomatoes

These have only become widely available fairly recently. They are small, firm, tasty and delicious raw, looking good mixed with coloured cherry tomatoes.

Coloured tomatoes

Yellow cherry tomatoes are often the sweetest and are usually best uncooked. Striped tomatoes add interest when mixed in with plain ones. Not all green tomatoes are unripe: some remain bright green when ripe and have a sharp, fresh taste. These are good mixed with red and yellow tomatoes. Lastly, you can get tomatoes that are so dark they look almost black.

56

Stems and leaves

Stems and leaves cannot be eaten, but for a strong, tomatoey smell you can add a piece of the stem to sauces and then remove it before serving.

Fresh or tinned?

When cooking, take into account which type of tomato it is best to use, but also consider whether to use fresh or tinned tomatoes. In Britain it is rarely possible to get good fresh tomatoes after November or before June. Most cooked dishes will taste better if you use good-quality tinned tomatoes rather than imports that have been grown in forced conditions or flown halfway round the world.

Health benefits

Tomatoes are rich in lycopene, an antioxidant that helps to protect against heart disease and cancer and may reduce the risk of appendicitis. They also contain beta-carotene, which is thought to fight cancer. Tomatoes are high in fibre, potassium, folic acid, vitamins A and C, and small amounts of vitamin E. Raw or grilled tomatoes contain the most nutrients, but if you cook them for a long time, some nutrients will be lost. On the downside, the leaves and stems are poisonous and the fruits are thought by some to aggravate arthritis and food allergies. On the beauty front, tomatoes help the circulation and maintain the elasticity of the skin – a face pack of tomato pulp and yoghurt is reputed to work wonders!

Buying fresh tomatoes

A good way to tell whether a tomato will be tasty is to
smell it. Make sure, though, that you are smelling the
tomato and not the vine (which has a much stronger
tomato scent). Vine-ripened tomatoes can be a bit of a
con as they rarely say how they were grown and the vine
itself has no effect on the flavour of the tomatoes.

However, it does indicate that the grower has been
prepared to take a certain amount of trouble
ripening his crop, so the tomatoes may have
had a better start in life. Above all, the
ones to be wary of are the packets
labelled 'grown for flavour' – most pre-
packaged tomatoes are grown for profit
and ease of transportation.

Storage

Never put tomatoes in a fridge. Temperatures below
10°C (50°F) harm not only the taste but also the
texture. Tomatoes don't even keep better in a fridge –
in fact soft ones will turn squishy faster. Most
supermarkets are kept unnaturally cold and purchased
tomatoes will improve in flavour after a couple of days.

For long-term storage, tomatoes are best frozen,
cooked or dried. In Britain it is extremely unlikely you
will be able to sun-dry your tomato crop, but you can
semi-dry or 'sunblush' them easily (see page 65).

Freezing tomatoes

Fresh tomatoes can be frozen. The best ones for freezing raw are those that are firm and just ripe. When thawed they will lose too much shape to be used in salads, but are excellent in cooked dishes. Remove the stalks and put small tomatoes straight into freezer bags, then freeze. Thaw for about 2 hours before use. Large tomatoes should be cut into wedges (beefsteaks are best quartered) and frozen in a single layer in a rigid container. They can be grilled or fried from frozen.

For frozen tomato juice, skin the tomatoes, chop roughly and simmer for about 10 minutes until soft. Sieve and leave to cool. Freeze in rigid containers and thaw for a couple of hours in the fridge before use.

For frozen tomato pureé, skin and chop the tomatoes as for juice, but continue to cook for about 30 minutes, until the pulp has reduced and thickened. Whizz in a blender if you wish. Cool and freeze in rigid containers. The purée can be thawed in the fridge or gently reheated in a heavy-bottomed saucepan.

To make frozen tomato sauce, skin and deseed the tomatoes and cook with onions, garlic and herbs of your choice. Season with salt, pepper and a little sugar if necessary. Simmer for about an hour, blend to a purée and allow to cool. Freeze in usable amounts in rigid containers and thaw as for purée.

Tomato products

Tinned tomatoes

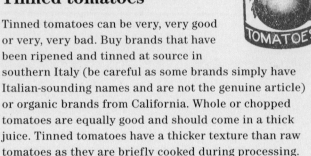

Tinned tomatoes can be very, very good or very, very bad. Buy brands that have been ripened and tinned at source in southern Italy (be careful as some brands simply have Italian-sounding names and are not the genuine article) or organic brands from California. Whole or chopped tomatoes are equally good and should come in a thick juice. Tinned tomatoes have a thicker texture than raw tomatoes as they are briefly cooked during processing. For dishes that require cooking for a long time, use the tomatoes and their juice; for rapidly cooked sauces, drain and reserve the juice for something else.

If the tomatoes look disappointing when you open the tin, add a teaspoon of sugar and a little tomato purée to improve the flavour, and a squeeze of lemon to get rid of the metallic taste.

Tomato ketchup

The original 'ketchup' was a seventeenth-century Chinese sauce made of pickled fish and spices. By the mid-eighteenth century it was popular in Britain, although tomatoes did not become the main ingredient until the 1800s. In 1876, Heinz tomato ketchup was launched with the slogan: 'Blessed relief for Mother and the other women in the household!'

Tomato purée

This comes in various concentrations and is simply tomato pulp which has been cooked until it is thick and strongly flavoured. Tubes can be stored in the fridge; tins should be decanted into a jar and covered with a thin layer of olive oil to prevent the formation of mould.

Passata

To make passata, tomatoes are cooked, pulped and sieved to produce a smooth, thick sauce. It is useful for soups, stews and sauces. Polpa is similar to passata, but is usually coarser.

Sun-dried tomatoes

The best sun-dried tomatoes come from hot, sunny Mediterranean countries where they have ripened fully in the sun and are then dried by it. Most commercially produced 'sun-dried' tomatoes are now dried in ovens. They are available either in jars of oil or totally dry in packets. Unless you find a bottled brand you particularly like, the packets are the best choice as you can select your own oil and flavours to add.

Mi-cuit tomatoes

These are semi-dried tomatoes from France. They do not need soaking and have an excellent strong flavour.

A word on the recipes

Many of the recipes here simply specify 'herbs': choose those that match the other dishes you are serving. Even where a particular herb is mentioned it is probably just because I like the dish cooked that way, and an alternative flavouring could almost certainly be substituted. Where possible, use fresh herbs. Depending on the herb, you can either cut it finely and sprinkle it over the tomatoes, or lay sprigs in amongst the tomatoes (rosemary and thyme are particularly suited to this). Many of the quantities are deliberately vague (handful, pinch), so you can use the amount you like.

I use olive oil, or a mixture of olive oil and butter, but again this is personal preference; in most cases, you could use sunflower oil instead. The amount of fat you use is, within reason, up to you and may depend on the type of pan. I have a very elderly frying pan that seems to soak up butter before I've even started cooking.

Eggs are large unless stated otherwise, and ideally free-range and organic. I use unsalted butter, full-cream milk and flat-leafed parsley (because I prefer it). Pepper is freshly ground and black.

I have not usually specified any particular varieties of tomato for these recipes, but in many cases a mixture of tomatoes is best. Each variety tastes subtly different, but they all complement each other.

Regard the recipes in this book as a starting point, altering and adding to them as you wish. Most are for four people, but some – particularly the salads – suggest four to six people.

Complementary flavours

The obvious herbs to pair with tomatoes are basil, chives, marjoram, mint, oregano, parsley, rosemary, sage, tarragon and thyme. It is better to add basil at the end. Marjoram is mild, suiting stuffed tomatoes and egg dishes. Sage also works well in stuffed tomatoes, while rosemary complements most meats. Less common partners are paprika and chilli for heat, cinnamon for sweetness, coriander leaf in salsas, and nutmeg (which can reduce any acidity).

Sugar emphasises the sweetness in tomatoes and helps bring out their flavour. Icing sugar is best for roast tomatoes, as it will melt easily without being stirred. Brown sugar will make the mixture richer and darker; for most dishes that are heated and stirred, caster sugar is best. Garlic, capers and olives complement almost all tomato dishes, with garlic being strongest raw and mildest as roasted cloves. Any member of the onion family will go well with tomatoes, as will any cheese, anchovies, bacon or eggs. In salads, balsamic vinegar is often the best choice for the dressing, as it will provide the balance of sweetness and acidity that tomatoes aspire to but don't always achieve.

Peeling, deseeding and slicing

Most raw tomatoes should not need peeling. Cooked tomatoes will eventually lose their skin and it is often better to get rid of it at the beginning, rather than have skins floating about on the plate. To peel tomatoes, make a small cross in the skin with a sharp knife and drop into boiling water. As soon as the skin begins to peel away, remove the tomato with a slotted spoon and put it into a bowl of cold water to stop it cooking. The skin should now peel away easily. The dunking in boiling water shouldn't last longer than about 20 seconds: you are loosening the skin, not cooking the tomato. If the skin looks really stubborn, it is better to use a sharp knife or peeler than boiling water.

The jelly around the seeds contains a lot of the flavour in tomatoes and if you scoop it all out, you run the risk of leaving yourself with a tasteless husk. That said, the jelly can make some dishes watery and the seeds tend to look unattractive. One solution is to push the seeds and jelly through a sieve or mouli and discard the seeds. If you are making a dish that requires a reasonable amount of cooking, the excess water in the jelly will evaporate anyway. For dishes such as stuffed tomatoes, you can simply spoon out the seeds and jelly and then stuff the cavity. For jellies and chutneys, it is useful to leave the seeds in as they contain pectin, which will improve the set.

The way you slice a tomato is largely a matter of common sense but, as a general rule, slice across for pizzas and salads and lengthways for wedges.

Roast tomatoes

For the best results when roasting tomatoes, either cook them fairly rapidly at a high temperature, as described here, or very slowly at a low one.

Heat the oven to 200°C/400°F/gas mark 6. Use plum or globe tomatoes if possible, and try to choose tomatoes that are roughly the same size. Halve the tomatoes (cut plum tomatoes lengthways) so they will cook evenly. Put them on a baking tray, cut side up, packing them closely together as they will shrink when they cook. Drizzle olive oil, salt, pepper and a little icing sugar over the top. Add some cloves of garlic or sprigs of thyme or rosemary, if you wish. Cook the tomatoes in the oven for 40–45 minutes (the exact time will depend on how ripe the tomatoes are) until they are very soft and slightly puffy.

Slow-roasted or sunblushed tomatoes

Preheat the oven to 110°C/225°F/gas mark ¼. Cherry tomatoes can be slow-roasted whole; larger tomatoes should be cut in half. Plum tomatoes are particularly good cut into quarters lengthways.

Spread out the tomatoes in a single layer on a baking tray. They can be closely packed, but ideally should not be touching. Drizzle with a little olive or sunflower oil, sprinkle with salt and a little icing sugar, and add torn basil leaves, oregano or thyme. Bake for 3 hours or longer, depending on how dry you want the tomatoes to be. Pack in jars with the oil and herbs from the baking

tray, adding more if necessary. Slow-roasted tomatoes
make perfect additions to soups, salads, pasta dishes
or sandwiches and they will keep for a couple of weeks
stored in the fridge.

If you live somewhere that is sufficiently sunny, you
can dry tomatoes in the sun to make 'sunblushed'
tomatoes. Cut the tomatoes in half and place face down
on a tray. Cover with gauze to protect the fruit from
insects and leave out in the sun. The weather obviously
needs to be dry and it helps if it is windy, as this will
speed up the drying process. Bring the tomatoes in
overnight to avoid the dew, store them somewhere
dry, and then put them out again the following day.
Depending on the weather, this process may take
several days.

Roast cherry tomatoes on the vine

These are the most accommodating tomatoes to roast, as
you can cook them at various temperatures to fit around
whatever else is in the oven.

Preheat the oven to anywhere between
180°C/350°F/gas mark 4 to 230°C/450°F/gas mark 8.
Oil a baking tray and lay the tomatoes on top, ensuring
that they are well coated in oil – drizzle a little more on
top if necessary. Sprinkle with salt, pepper and icing
sugar. Add cloves of garlic or sprigs of herbs in between
the trusses if you wish. Cook the tomatoes for 10
minutes at a high heat, or for 30–40 minutes at a lower
temperature. Remove from the tray carefully so that the
trusses don't fall apart.

Grilled tomatoes

Grilled tomatoes take longer to cook than you might imagine, although the exact time obviously depends on the size and ripeness of the tomatoes. Cut the tomatoes in half and drizzle a little olive oil over them. Season with salt, pepper and herbs. Grill under a high heat to seal them and then continue under a lower heat to ensure that they are cooked right through.

Fried tomatoes

Small tomatoes are best cut in half and fried face-down, whereas larger ones cook better in chunky slices. Fry at a high temperature to start with, to seal the tomatoes, and then at a lower temperature until cooked right through. The fat you use is a matter of personal preference, but oil and garlic, or bacon fat, are especially good.

Tomatoes chargrill beautifully, either on a barbecue or griddle pan. Again, ensure that they are cooked right through and don't have raw centres.

Fresh tomato sauce

You can make a sauce from either fresh or tinned tomatoes. If your fresh tomatoes are very good, they can be used raw; alternatively, cook them for as short a time as possible. Less good tomatoes need to be cooked for about 40 minutes to give the acidic juices time to seep out and evaporate. When fresh tomatoes are out of season, use good-quality tinned tomatoes.

SERVES 4 (AS A PASTA SAUCE)

600G (1LB 5OZ) TOMATOES, PEELED AND DESEEDED, OR 1 X 400G TIN
  TOMATOES, DRAINED AND CHOPPED
1 CLOVE GARLIC, CRUSHED
HANDFUL OF BASIL LEAVES, TORN
½ TBSP OREGANO, CHOPPED
OLIVE OIL
SALT AND PEPPER

TO SERVE

COOKED PASTA
PARMESAN CHEESE

Chop the tomatoes finely. Mix the tomatoes, garlic, basil and oregano together in a bowl. Add sufficient olive oil to hold it all together. Season with salt and pepper: you may need quite a lot of salt, depending on the tomatoes. Mix well and leave to stand for about 20–30 minutes so that the flavours can develop.

Stir the sauce into hot pasta and serve with freshly grated Parmesan cheese sprinkled over the top.

Creamy tomato sauce

This is an indulgent sauce that goes well with pasta, white fish or chicken.

SERVES 4 (AS A PASTA SAUCE)

50G (1¾OZ) BUTTER

1 ONION, FINELY CHOPPED

450G (1LB) TOMATOES, PEELED, DESEEDED AND CHOPPED, OR 1 X 400G
   TIN TOMATOES, DRAINED AND CHOPPED

JUICE OF 1 LEMON

300ML (½ PINT) DOUBLE CREAM

HANDFUL OF SMALL BASIL LEAVES

SALT AND PEPPER

Melt the butter in a large, heavy-bottomed frying pan and cook the onion gently, until transparent.

Add the tomatoes and lemon juice and cook until the tomato is just soft. Stir in the cream, mix well and simmer until the sauce reduces and thickens (the length of time will depend on how juicy the tomatoes are and how thick you want the sauce to be).

Season with salt and pepper. For a really smooth sauce, blitz with a hand-held blender. Add the basil at the last minute – this sauce looks particularly attractive with small, whole basil leaves.

Creamy tomato soup

You can use any type of tomatoes for this soup, but they must be just ripe and full of flavour. Do not use stock cubes: they will ruin the flavour of the soup. Bouillon powder or ready-made liquid stock is fine. Chicken or vegetable stock will complement tomatoes without overpowering them.

SERVES 2–3

50G (1¾OZ) UNSALTED BUTTER

1 ONION, FINELY CHOPPED

1 CLOVE GARLIC, FINELY CHOPPED

2 TSP MIXED DRIED HERBS

PINCH OF POWDERED CHILLI (OPTIONAL)

300ML (½ PINT) STOCK (SEE ABOVE)

1KG (2¼ LB) FRESH TOMATOES

80ML (3FL OZ) DOUBLE CREAM

SALT, PEPPER AND CASTER SUGAR

BASIL OR PARSLEY

Melt the butter in a heavy-bottomed frying pan and fry the onion, garlic, herbs and chilli (if using) for a few minutes until soft. Add the stock and the tomatoes. Bring to the boil, cover with a lid and simmer for 15 minutes.

Leave the soup to cool slightly and then liquidise in a blender. Push the mixture through a sieve, reheat and season to taste with salt, pepper and sugar. Stir in the cream and reheat gently: do not allow to boil.

Garnish with torn basil or parsley. Serve with crusty bread.

Gazpacho

This chilled soup is best made with really good, sun-ripened tomatoes from the garden. Serve the soup very cold on a hot day. It keeps well and is, if anything, better the following day.

SERVES 4–6

1 RED PEPPER

2–3 THICK SLICES OF DAY-OLD GOOD WHITE BREAD, CRUSTS REMOVED, TORN INTO CHUNKS

OLIVE OIL

1KG (2¼ LB) TOMATOES, PEELED, DESEEDED AND ROUGHLY CHOPPED

1 LARGE SPANISH ONION, CHOPPED

¾ CUCUMBER, PEELED AND CHOPPED

2 LARGE CLOVES GARLIC, CRUSHED

2–3 TBSP RED OR WHITE WINE VINEGAR

150ML (5FL OZ) TOMATO JUICE

SALT, PEPPER AND CASTER SUGAR

Preheat the grill. Cut the pepper into quarters and remove the seeds. Grill until the skin blackens, allow to cool briefly and then peel the skin away and discard. Chop roughly and put in a bowl.

Add the bread and pour in olive oil until the bread is just saturated. Add the tomatoes, onion, cucumber, garlic, vinegar and tomato juice. Season with salt, pepper and, if necessary, a little sugar. Blitz all the ingredients in a blender until smooth.

Add iced water until the soup is the required consistency, check the seasoning and chill until required. Ladle into bowls and garnish with chopped spring onion, hard-boiled eggs, red pepper, cucumber or cherry tomatoes.

Pizza Margherita

In 1899, the king and queen of Italy visited Naples. Queen Margherita particularly wanted to try pizza, the local speciality, and was offered a patriotic topping of tomato, mozzarella cheese and basil, echoing the red, white and green of the Italian flag. It was named after the queen in honour of her visit. For this recipe, hard mozzarella is better than the balls of cheese that are sold in water, as it doesn't go soggy.

MAKES TWO 23CM (9IN) PIZZAS

FOR THE BASE

350G (12OZ) PLAIN FLOUR

½ TSP SALT

7G SACHET EASY-BLEND DRIED YEAST

1 TBSP MILK

2 TBSP OLIVE OIL

FOR THE TOMATO SAUCE

1 TBSP OLIVE OIL

1 X 400G TIN TOMATOES, WHOLE OR CHOPPED

1 CLOVE GARLIC, PEELED AND LEFT WHOLE

OREGANO, TO TASTE

SALT AND PEPPER

FOR THE TOPPING

150G (5½OZ) HARD MOZZARELLA CHEESE, GRATED

1 TBSP GRATED PARMESAN CHEESE

HANDFUL OF BASIL LEAVES, TORN

OLIVE OIL

Preheat the oven to 220°C/425°F/gas mark 7. To make the base, put the ingredients in a big bowl. Add 150ml (5fl oz) warm water and mix to give a firm dough. Add more water or flour as necessary. Knead on a flat surface for 10 minutes. Put in an oiled bowl, cover with a damp cloth and set aside for 30 minutes.

To make the sauce, heat the oil in a saucepan and add the tomatoes, garlic clove and oregano. Break up the tomatoes and cook for about 20 minutes until the mixture has reduced to a thick sludge. Remove the garlic clove. Season with salt and pepper to taste.

Grease a large baking tray (or two). Turn out the dough, flatten it and cut it in half. Put each piece on the baking tray and roll or press into a circle roughly 23cm (9in) in diameter. Leave to rise in a warm place for 5–10 minutes.

Spread a thin layer of tomato sauce on each pizza base. Do not be tempted to use too much. There will be some left over, but this can be served separately for dipping the crusts in. Spread the cheeses over the pizzas and sprinkle with the torn basil leaves. Drizzle with olive oil. Bake for about 20 minutes, until the base of each pizza is crisp.

Variations
• Add 1 tsp thyme to the tomato mixture.
• Include additional toppings such as anchovies, pepperoni, prosciutto, ham, capers, black olives or artichoke hearts.
• Scatter basil, rocket or baby spinach leaves on the pizza when it comes out of the oven.

Aubergine parmigiana

This makes an excellent supper served with a green salad and crusty bread, and washed down with some red wine.

SERVES 4

900G (2LB) AUBERGINES
OLIVE OIL
2 LARGE ONIONS, FINELY CHOPPED
2 CLOVES GARLIC, CRUSHED
1 X 400G TIN TOMATOES, CHOPPED
225G (8OZ) MOZZARELLA CHEESE, SLICED
6 TBSP GRATED PARMESAN CHEESE
SALT AND PEPPER

Slice the aubergines into circles 5mm (¼ in) thick. It used to be best to salt aubergines to remove the bitterness, but this is rarely necessary with modern varieties. However, it is still worth salting them to stop them soaking up too much oil. Spread out the slices in a dish, sprinkle lightly with salt and leave for 30–60 minutes. Pat dry.

Preheat the oven to 200°C/400°F/gas mark 6. Heat the oil in a large frying pan and fry the onion and garlic for about 10 minutes. Remove from the pan with a slotted spoon and fry the aubergine until crisp and lightly browned, adding more oil if necessary. Layer the aubergines, onion, tomatoes and mozzarella cheese in an ovenproof dish, sprinkling Parmesan, salt and pepper between the layers. Finish with a layer of aubergines.

Bake uncovered for 40–60 minutes, until the aubergines are cooked through and tender.

Feta, olive and tomato tart

This is an attractive tart combining the clear and simple flavours
of tomatoes, feta cheese and olives. Don't stint on the quality of the
ingredients: tasteless tomatoes, bland feta cheese or dull olives will
ruin the meal!

SERVES 4–6

4 TBSP OLIVE OIL

HANDFUL OF BASIL LEAVES

BAKED 20CM (8IN) PASTRY CASE*

400G (14OZ) FIRM FETA CHEESE

4–5 LARGE TOMATOES, SLICED

HANDFUL OF BLACK OLIVES, STONED IF YOU WISH

SALT AND PEPPER

* To prepare the pastry case, line a 20cm (8in) tart tin with
shortcrust pastry and bake it blind.

Mix the olive oil and basil leaves in a jar and leave for a couple
of hours or overnight.

Preheat the oven to 190°C/375°F/gas mark 5. Crumble the
cheese over the base of the pastry case. Arrange the tomatoes
on top in concentric rings, interspersed evenly with the olives.
Drizzle a little of the herb-infused oil over the top and season
with salt and pepper.

Bake for 45 minutes, until the pastry is golden and the
tomatoes are cooked.

Middle Eastern stuffed tomatoes

You can put almost any leftovers into a tomato, such as shepherd's pie, risotto or any cheese. Beefsteak tomatoes are the best ones to use: they should be ripe but firm, and able to stand squarely on a dish.

SERVES 4

1 TBSP CURRANTS
1 TBSP RED WINE VINEGAR
4 LARGE TOMATOES
OLIVE OIL
1 ONION, CHOPPED
250G (9OZ) MINCED BEEF OR LAMB
1 TSP ZA'ATAR, 1 TSP DUQQA OR
  ½ TSP GROUND CINNAMON
½–1 TSP CHILLI SAUCE, DEPENDING HOW HOT YOU WANT THE FILLING
HANDFUL OF FLAT-LEAF PARSLEY
SALT AND PEPPER

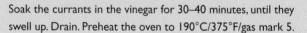

Soak the currants in the vinegar for 30–40 minutes, until they swell up. Drain. Preheat the oven to 190°C/375°F/gas mark 5.

Cut the top off each tomato to form a lid and set aside. Scoop out the centre of the tomatoes and discard.

Heat the olive oil and fry the onion until golden, then add the meat and cook until brown. Add the currants, spice, chilli sauce and parsley. Season to taste with salt and pepper.

Press the mixture into the tomatoes and put the lids back on. Pack the tomatoes tightly in an oiled baking dish, drizzle a little oil on top and bake for about 35 minutes.

Tomato risotto

This risotto is delicious as it is, or you could add fresh vegetables such as courgettes or peas, or meat such as ham or meatballs.

SERVES 4

BUTTER AND OLIVE OIL

1 ONION, FINELY CHOPPED

675G (1LB 7OZ) RIPE PLUM TOMATOES, PEELED AND DICED (IF THERE
    ARE A LOT OF SEEDS, REMOVE MOST OF THEM)

1–2 TBSP TOMATO PURÉE

300G (11OZ) ARBORIO RICE

1.5 LITRES (2½ PINTS) HOT VEGETABLE STOCK

75G (3OZ) PARMESAN CHEESE, FRESHLY GRATED

SALT AND PEPPER

Heat the butter and the oil in a large, heavy frying pan (the percentages of each doesn't matter). Fry the onion until transparent and soft. Add the tomatoes and tomato purée, season and cook over a medium heat for about 5 minutes, stirring.

Add the rice and mix thoroughly so it is well coated. Add a little stock and stir until the liquid has mostly been absorbed. Continue adding the stock gradually, stirring and scraping the bottom of the pan so the rice does not stick. After about 25–30 minutes, the rice should be tender and the stock used up.

Remove from the heat, stir in a knob of butter and half the cheese. Season to taste with salt and pepper. Allow the risotto to rest for a few minutes and then serve with the rest of the cheese.

Greek salad

The quality of the ingredients is everything in a salad: use perfectly ripe tomatoes and good extra-virgin olive oil.

Serves 4–6

1 CUCUMBER, PEELED AND CUT INTO CHUNKS

4–6 LARGE TOMATOES, CUT INTO CHUNKS

12 BLACK OLIVES, STONED

1 TSP CHOPPED OREGANO

115G (4OZ) FETA CHEESE, DICED

For the dressing

JUICE OF ½ LEMON

EXTRA-VIRGIN OLIVE OIL

SALT AND PEPPER

First, make the dressing. Put the lemon juice and oil in a jar, seal, shake well and season with salt and pepper.

Put the cucumber and tomato chunks in a large bowl. Add the olives and most of the oregano and mix well. Drizzle the dressing over the salad. Add the diced feta, sprinkle the remaining oregano on top and serve immediately.

Insalata tricolore

This is another easy salad and, like the Greek Salad opposite, depends on the quality of the ingredients for good results. If you want to conjure up the experience of eating an al fresco meal overlooking an Italian beach, you will need big, tasty tomatoes, proper buffalo mozzarella cheese, and ripe but firm avocados. It is important that this salad looks pretty, so cut up everything neatly.

SERVES 6

6 LARGE TOMATOES, SLICED HORIZONTALLY
3 MOZZARELLA CHEESES, THICKLY SLICED
3 AVOCADOS, PEELED AND SLICED
EXTRA-VIRGIN OLIVE OIL
JUICE OF 1 LEMON
BASIL LEAVES
SALT AND PEPPER

Arrange the tomato, mozzarella and avocado slices on a large platter. Drizzle with the oil and lemon juice. Season with salt and pepper, and decorate with basil leaves. Leave the salad to sit for a little while to allow the flavours to develop, but be careful as the avocado will turn brown if left for too long.

Panzanella

Italian bread (such as ciabatta) and ripe plum tomatoes are the crucial ingredients in this salad. Apart from that, it would traditionally have been made with whatever was to hand – cucumber, roasted red peppers, black olives, celery, capers and anchovies.

SERVES 4–6

10 LARGE RIPE TOMATOES

2 CLOVES GARLIC, CRUSHED

4 TBSP OLIVE OIL

1 TBSP RED WINE VINEGAR

2 RED PEPPERS, CHARGRILLED AND PEELED (SEE PAGE 71)

1 CUCUMBER, DESEEDED AND CHOPPED

HANDFUL OF CAPERS, RINSED AND DRAINED

1 SMALL TIN ANCHOVIES, DRAINED

HANDFUL OF BASIL OR PARSLEY

1 LOAF OF GOOD DAY-OLD WHITE BREAD

SALT AND PEPPER

Peel the tomatoes. Scoop out the jelly and seeds and sieve these to extract the juice, which has lots of flavour. Mix the juice with the garlic, oil and vinegar. Season with salt and pepper.

Cut the tomatoes into chunks and slice the peppers into strips. Put into a large bowl with the cucumber, pour in the dressing and toss. Add the capers and anchovies. Scatter the herbs over the salad. Leave for about half an hour before serving.

Tear the bread into small chunks, toast lightly and mix into the salad just before serving.

Beans in tomato and cream sauce

This recipe is based on one by Sophie Grigson, which she included in both her Book of Ingredients *and* Taste of the Times *because it is so delicious. These beans are far removed from the tinned baked variety, but can be used in much the same way. Serve with sausages, bacon or lamb chops, or reduce the cream and serve with fried eggs. You can use fresh plum tomatoes or tinned ones.*

SERVES 4

30G (1OZ) BUTTER

1 SMALL ONION, FINELY CHOPPED

1 X 400G TIN TOMATOES, ROUGHLY CHOPPED OR 500G (1LB 2OZ) FRESH
   PLUM TOMATOES, PEELED AND CHOPPED INTO CHUNKS

1 TBSP TOMATO PURÉE

1 LARGE SPRIG OF FRESH ROSEMARY

GENEROUS PINCH OF SUGAR

1 X 400G TIN FLAGEOLET BEANS

150ML (5FL OZ) DOUBLE CREAM

SALT AND PEPPER

Melt the butter in a frying pan and fry the onion gently until soft. Add the tomatoes, tomato purée, rosemary and sugar. Season with salt and pepper. Simmer for 10 minutes. Remove the rosemary.

Drain and rinse the beans. Add the cream and beans to the tomato mixture. Season with salt and pepper, if necessary, and heat through but do not boil.

81

Bruschetta

The essentials here are good bread, well-flavoured olive oil and sweet, ripe tomatoes. Use small cherry tomatoes or any larger tomatoes, as long as they are juicy.

RUSTIC WHITE BREAD, THICKLY SLICED

GARLIC CLOVES, PEELED AND CUT IN HALF LENGTHWAYS

CHERRY TOMATOES, HALVED, OR LARGER TOMATOES, PEELED AND
   CUT INTO CHUNKS

OLIVE OIL

BASIL

SALT AND PEPPER

Grill the bread on both sides. While it is still hot, rub one side with garlic and then squash the tomatoes into the bread. Drizzle a little oil on the top and season with salt and pepper. Garnish with torn basil leaves and serve while the bread is still warm.

Tomato ice

This makes a good summer starter. It is prepared in advance and frozen, then removed from the freezer and piled into dishes just before serving. This is very quick and easy to do; if you have guests, they will hardly notice your absence.

SERVES 6

1.5KG (3LB 2OZ) RIPE TOMATOES, ROUGHLY CHOPPED

½ RED ONION, FINELY CHOPPED

HANDFUL OF THYME OR MARJORAM, CHOPPED

1 TBSP TOMATO PURÉE

JUICE OF 1 LEMON

CASTER SUGAR TO TASTE

TO SERVE

½ CUCUMBER, PEELED AND FINELY SLICED

MINT

LEMON WEDGES

Put the tomatoes, onion and herbs in a large saucepan and bring to the boil. Cover and simmer gently for 25 minutes, stirring, until the tomatoes are soft. Sieve the tomatoes and mix with the tomato purée, lemon juice and sugar.

Leave to cool and spoon into a plastic container. Cover with a lid and freeze for about 4 hours until solid.

Line six glass dishes with overlapping slices of cucumber. Turn the tomato mixture out and crush it with a rolling pin. Pile the tomato ice into the dishes, garnish with mint and serve with wedges of lemon.

Prosciutto tartlets

These tartlets are very pretty. They make perfect nibbles, starters or picnic food.

MAKES 12

ABOUT 6 SLICES OF PROSCIUTTO

12 MEDIUM EGGS

12 CHERRY TOMATOES, HALVED

2 TBSP CHIVES, CHOPPED

2 TBSP CREAM

4 TBSP GRATED PARMESAN CHEESE

SALT AND PEPPER

Preheat the oven to 180°C/350°F/gas mark 4. Lightly oil a 12-hole muffin tray. Cut the prosciutto into strips and lay over the base and sides of each hole. Three strips should be sufficient for each one – it doesn't matter if there are a few gaps.

Break an egg into each prosciutto cup, drop in two cherry tomato halves and sprinkle with chives. Drizzle with cream, season with salt and pepper and scatter the Parmesan on top.

Bake for 15–20 minutes, until the egg is just set and starting to pull away from the sides. Leave to cool for 5 minutes. Run a knife around each mould to loosen the tartlet and remove to a wire tray. Eat warm or at room temperature.

Cherry tomato canapés

The crucial thing here is the size of the tomatoes: they need to be small enough to remain bite-sized, but large enough to hold a reasonable amount of filling – about 2cm (¾in) across is perfect.

MAKES 20

10 RIPE CHERRY TOMATOES

SMALL POT OF WHITE CRABMEAT

3–4 TBSP MAYONNAISE

TABASCO SAUCE

SQUIRT OF LEMON JUICE

1 TBSP FINELY CHOPPED BASIL

SALT AND PEPPER

Cut each tomato in half horizontally and scoop out the seeds. Line a plate with kitchen paper and lay the tomatoes, cut side down, on the paper for 30 minutes to drain.

Mix together the crabmeat, mayonnaise, a few drops of Tabasco and a squirt of lemon juice. Season to taste. Fill each tomato and sprinkle with basil.

ALTERNATIVE FILLINGS

• Guacamole with a tablespoon of finely chopped coriander to garnish.

• Soft cream cheese mixed with fresh herbs (basil, parsley, chives or marjoram) and black pepper.

Tomato bread

Libby Kerr, one of my brilliant testers, won first prize with this in the 'Savoury Bread' class at her local show! The recipe calls for sun-dried tomatoes: some types are sold preserved in olive oil, but others are just sold dry. If you are using dry tomatoes, soak them in olive oil first so they soften up. When you add the tomatoes to the bread mixture, they should be in about 2 tablespoons of oil.

MAKES 1 LOAF

500G (1LB 2OZ) STRONG WHITE FLOUR

1 TSP SALT

7G SACHET EASY-BLEND DRIED YEAST

1 TBSP TOMATO PURÉE

6 SUN-DRIED TOMATOES (SEE NOTE ABOVE), CHOPPED OR WHIZZED BRIEFLY
IN A BLENDER

12 BLACK OLIVES, STONED AND CHOPPED (OPTIONAL)

300ML (½ PINT) TEPID WATER

HANDFUL OF ROSEMARY

Put the flour, salt, yeast, tomato purée, tomatoes and olives (if using) into a large bowl and mix well. Pour in the water gradually, mixing well, until you have a dough that is soft and workable but not sticky.

Turn the dough on to a floured work surface and knead for about 10 minutes. Shape the dough into a round and put it in a greased bowl, turning it so it is well coated in fat. Cover the bowl with a damp tea towel and leave in a warm place. After 1½–2 hours, it should have doubled in size.

Punch the dough down, remove it from the bowl and knead gently for a minute. Grease a large baking tray and shape the dough into a loaf on it (long or round, whichever you prefer). Push small sprigs of rosemary into the surface, cover with a tea towel and leave for another 30 minutes to rise again.

Preheat the oven to 230°C/450°F/gas mark 8. Bake the bread for 10 minutes and then reduce the temperature to 200°C/400°F/gas mark 6 for another 15–20 minutes. The loaf should be nicely risen and golden, and should sound hollow when tapped. Remove from the oven and cool on a wire rack.

Green tomato chutney

*The quantities here are very flexible. The amount of sugar needed
will depend on the sweetness of the tomatoes and apples, so add it
gradually and taste as you go. If the tomato skins are hard to remove,
use a vegetable peeler.*

MAKES ABOUT 6 JARS OF CHUTNEY

450ML (¾ PINT) RED WINE VINEGAR OR CIDER VINEGAR
700G (1½LB) GREEN TOMATOES, PEELED AND CHOPPED INTO CHUNKS
350G (12OZ) FIRM EATING APPLES, PEELED, CORED AND CUT INTO CHUNKS
350G (12OZ) ONIONS, CHOPPED
200G (7OZ) RAISINS, CHOPPED
2 TSP GRATED FRESH GINGER
1 TSP GROUND ALLSPICE
2 CLOVES GARLIC, CRUSHED
300G (11OZ) SUGAR, GOLDEN GRANULATED OR DARK BROWN
SALT AND PEPPER

Put half the vinegar and everything else except for the sugar into
a large, heavy pan. Season with salt and pepper. Bring to the boil
and simmer for 1 hour. Stir occasionally, especially towards the
end when it has a tendency to stick.

Add the rest of the vinegar and gradually add the sugar.
Simmer the mixture for another hour until it becomes jelly-like
and drops off a spoon in a reasonably cohesive dollop.

Spoon the chutney into warm, sterilised jars. Remove any spills
from the jars and label them. Ideally, the chutney should be stored
in a cool, dark place for a month to allow the flavours to develop.

Tomato jelly

This is a very beautiful, slightly grainy jelly and makes an excellent accompaniment to cold meat and cheese, especially goat's cheese. The version below is quite sweet and goes well with sharp cheese; for a less sweet, more lemony jelly, use 3–4 tbsp of lemon juice for each 600ml (1 pint) of juice.

MAKES ABOUT 2 JARS OF JELLY

900G (2LB) TOMATOES, CHOPPED
GRANULATED SUGAR
LEMON JUICE (SEE ABOVE)

Put a couple of saucers in the fridge to cool. Put the tomatoes into a food processor and blitz until they form a pulp. Push through a sieve and measure the juice.

Adding 400g (14oz) sugar and 2 tbsp lemon juice for each 600ml (1 pint) of juice, put everything into a large, heavy-bottomed pan and heat gently until the sugar has dissolved. Bring to the boil and cook rapidly until setting point is reached. To test for this, remove the pan from the heat as soon as the jelly seems to thicken (you can always cook the jelly a bit more if you find it hasn't reached setting point, but you cannot 'uncook' it if it goes too far). Put a dollop of the jelly on a saucer and as it cools, push your finger through it: a wrinkly skin will form on the surface if it has reached setting point.

Pour the tomato jelly into warm, sterilised jars, seal and label once cool.

National Trust kitchen gardens

Many kitchen gardens in country houses now owned by the National Trust have been restored to their former glory, supplying the cafes and restaurants at the properties and providing a surplus for sale.

The gardens listed below all grow interesting and inspirational vegetables. Many have greenhouses: there isn't always access for the public but you can usually peek in. Other properties have kitchen gardens too, and it is also worth checking with the National Trust for the latest news as gardens are being restored all the time.

Further information on the gardens and their opening times can be found in the National Trust Handbook or at www.nationaltrust.org.uk.

Alfriston Clergy House, Alfriston, Polegate, East Sussex. The little kitchen garden has the feel of a domestic garden, with hedges on three sides and views over the River Cuckmere.

Apprentice House, Quarry Bank Mill, Styal, Cheshire. The Apprentice House housed 100 child labourers who worked in the adjoining mill, built in 1784. The re-created plots show the food the children grew for themselves and for sale.

Arlington Court, Barnstaple, Devon. The kitchen garden has been restored with greenhouses, vegetables, flowers and fruit.

Barrington Court, near Ilminster, Somerset. The walled kitchen garden has flower borders beneath a pumpkin arch.

Bateman's, Burwash, East Sussex. The kitchen garden is alongside the orchard. There are also vegetables in the borders of the mulberry garden, planted as they would have been in Rudyard Kipling's time.

Beningbrough Hall, Beningbrough, York. The walled kitchen garden has a pear alley with flowers beneath. Vegetables and flowers are planted in deep beds around the walls.

Calke Abbey, Ticknall, Derby. The Physic Garden has been restored as a kitchen garden, with rotating beds of old varieties.

Clumber Park, Worksop, Nottinghamshire. The walled kitchen garden has a huge range of twelve interconnected glasshouses.

The Courts Garden, Holt, near Bradford-on-Avon, Wiltshire. The recently restored kitchen garden includes herb borders, pear espaliers, a nuttery, an orchard and an apple arch.

Felbrigg Hall, Felbrigg, Norwich, Norfolk. The walled kitchen garden is a fully working garden.

Fenton House, Hampstead, London. This town house has a charming, country-style orchard and vegetable garden.

Ham House, Ham, Richmond-upon-Thames, Surrey. The seventeenth-century walled garden consists of sixteen rectangular areas, four of which are now the kitchen garden.

Hidcote, Hidcote Bartrim, near Chipping Campden, Gloucestershire. The winter of 2008–9 saw the beginning of a three-year restoration of the kitchen garden.

Hinton Ampner, near Alresford, Hampshire. The walled garden has been restored and is attractive and productive.

Hughenden Manor, High Wycombe, Buckinghamshire. The Victorian walled kitchen garden has a wonderful mixture of vegetables, fruit and flowers in different growing conditions.

Kingston Lacy, Wimbourne Minster, Dorset. This 6-acre site will eventually be home to 80 allotments, containing everything from pigs to sunflowers. The old glasshouses and cold frames are being restored.

Knightshayes Court, Bolham, Tiverton, Devon. The Victorian walled garden is surrounded by beautiful stone walls with turrets at the corners.

Llanerchaeron, Ciliau Aeron, near Aberaeron, Ceredigion. This has been cultivated for ten generations. There are raised beds to counter the problems of the high rainfall.

Monk's House, Rodmell, Lewes, East Sussex. A gap in the hedge leads through to a large area of six allotments. Each is slightly different in approach, but they all fit together as a pleasing whole, with flowers in amongst vegetables.

Nunnington Hall, Nunnington, near York. The small, attractive vegetable and cutting garden uses comfrey tea as a fertiliser.

Osterley Park, Isleworth, Middlesex. The Tudor walled garden is partly laid out as a cutting patch, with neat rows of plants. The remaining area contains four huge beds of flowers and vegetables grown ornamentally. The amazing result is a cross between a Gauguin painting and Alice's Wonderland.

Packwood House, Lapworth, Warwickshire. The restoration of the walled kitchen garden is a work in progress and the area is a beautiful balance of old and new, in terms of both plants and structures.

Sissinghurst Castle, near Cranbrook, Kent. The vegetable garden is large and practical, rather than ornamental.

Snowshill Manor, Snowshill, near Broadway, Gloucestershire. The attractive kitchen garden is surrounded by low stone walls and has a mixture of vegetables, fruit and flowers.

Stourhead, Stourton, Warminster, Wiltshire. The walled garden at this property is divided into three parts. There are fruit trees, vegetables and flowers, and interesting old underground brick water tanks as well. There is a farm shop and a good garden blog (http://trustgardening.wordpress.com/).

Tintinhull Garden, Tintinhull, Yeovil, Somerset. There is an attractive kitchen garden, which has the feel of a cottage garden, producing the amounts needed for a small house.

Trengwainton Garden, Madron, near Penzance. Each of the five walled gardens has a separate theme: fruit, vegetables, ornamental planting, a pumpkin patch and a community garden.

Tyntesfield, Wraxall, Bristol, Somerset. The kitchen gardens have remained in continuous cultivation since at least 1837. There is a large walled garden and a huge range of glasshouses.

Upton House, near Banbury, Warwickshire. There is a large kitchen garden within a valley which is hidden from the main lawn by a ha-ha. The flowers, fruit and vegetables cascade down a slope to the Mirror Pool at the bottom.

The Vyne, Sherbourne St John, Basingstoke, Hampshire. Part of the large walled garden has been restored as a productive garden, with vegetable and cutting beds and glasshouses.

Westbury Court Garden, Westbury-on-Severn, Gloucestershire. This Dutch water garden, laid out between 1695 and 1705, has an area of fruit, vegetable and herb plots with period plants.

Wimpole Hall, Arrington, Royston, Cambridgeshire. The walled kitchen garden was restored largely by volunteers and has vegetables, flowers, espaliered fruit and a large glasshouse.

The Workhouse, Southwell, Nottinghamshire. This is a nineteenth-century workhouse. The re-created garden shows what paupers would have eaten at the time.

Tomato Days

Many National Trust gardens hold tomato festivals, usually in late August or early September when most tomatoes are ripening; for example Wimpole Hall (see the National Trust website for other details).

An organisation called Garden Organic (formerly the Henry Doubleday Research Institute) celebrates Tomato Day at its garden at Ryton in Warwickshire. This idea has been taken up by many allotment societies, nurseries and organic groups around the country. See www.gardenorganic.co.uk for details.

British Tomato Week is in late May, in time to encourage us to plant tomatoes. For further information, visit www.britishtomatoes.co.uk. A tomato festival called Totally Tomatoes is held at West Dean Gardens in West Sussex in early September. See www.westdean.org.uk.

At a tomato festival (La Tomatina) held in Valencia in late August in honour of St Louis Bertrand, a sixteenth-century missionary, vast numbers of people gather and throw overripe tomatoes at each other.

Picture credits

pages 15, 16, 17, 18, 30, 36, 43, 66, 76 © Becca Thorne

page 5 INTERFOTO / Bildarchiv Hansmann / Mary Evans Picture Library

pages 9, 21 © Beryl Peters Collection / Alamy

pages 11, 33, 85 Images courtesy of The Advertising Archives

pages 24, 45 © Cynthia Hart Designer / Corbis

pages 46, 50 © Amoret Tanner / Alamy

page 48 © amana images inc. / Alamy

pages 53, 63 © PoodlesRock/Corbis

page 70 Mary Evans Picture Library

page 87 © Swim Ink 2, LLC/CORBIS

Index